family
of
liars

e.lockhart

HOT
KEY
BOOKS

First published in Great Britain in 2022 by Hot Key Books

This edition published in 2023 by
HOT KEY BOOKS
4th Floor, Victoria House, Bloomsbury Square
London WC1B 4DA
Owned by Bonnier Books
Sveavägen 56, Stockholm, Sweden
www.hotkeybooks.com

Published by arrangement with Random House Children's Books,
a division of Penguin Random House LLC

A CIP catalogue record for this book is available from the British Library.

ISBN: 978-1-4714-1352-0
Exclusive edition ISBN: 978-1-4714-1480-0
Also available as an ebook and in audio

1

The text of this book is set in 11-point Joanna MT.
Interior design by Ken Crossland
Printed and bound in Great Britain by Clays Ltd, Elcograf S.p.A.

Hot Key Books is an imprint of Bonnier Books UK
www.bonnierbooks.co.uk